A Ride for Duck

By **KELLY NOGOSKI** and **LESLIE FALCONER**   Illustrated by **KELLY NOGOSKI**

First published by Experience Early Learning Company
7243 Scotchwood Lane, Grawn, Michigan 49637 USA

ISBN 978-1-937954-28-4
visit us at **www.ExperienceEarlyLearning.com**

This is Duck.

Duck loves
the muck.
He also loves
to drive his ...

... motorcycle.

But today,
Duck's out of luck.
First his motorcycle
got a flat tire,
then he stepped
on a (dangerous)
wire!

"I need to buy some foot cream!" he cried.

"If only I could find a ride."

"Oh good," said Duck. "Here comes Goat. She'll give me a ride in her shiny blue ...

... boat."

I'm a duck out of luck. Can you please give me a ride?

Duck pleads,
but Goat clears
her throat.
"Sorry, but I must
deliver a note."

Dearest Chicken,
Thank you for the
lovely hat. I like
to wear it while
driving my boat.
Hope everything is
great on the farm.
Sincerely,
Goat

"Fiddlesticks," says Duck, then looks up and spots Wayne. You know, the lion with the giant mane? He's flying high in his two-seater ...

... airplane!

I'm a duck out of luck. Can you please give me a ride?

Duck pleads,
but Wayne
starts to explain,
"Sorry my friend,
it's about to rain."

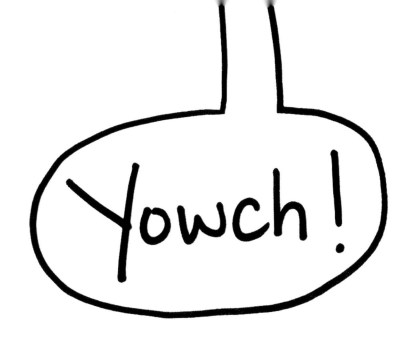

"Fiddlesticks,"
says Duck,
and kicks the dirt,
which starts to make
his other foot hurt.

Feeling hopeless,
Duck sits down.
The cold, wet rain
falls all around.
Oh, but what's this?
Could it be Mike,
the friendly pike
on his tiny ...

... bike?

I have the need for speed.

Duck pleads,
but Mike
blubbers and says,
"I'm sorry my friend,
as much as I'd like,
you are just too big
for my bike."

Duck starts to cry
with great emotion.

Goat, Wayne and Mike are puzzled indeed. Doesn't Duck know he has what he needs?

"Duck," they say,
"look over there,
in the garage.
No need to despair.
You're not out of luck
and definitely
not stuck. Remember,
Duck, you have a ...

... truck!"

"Silly me!"
Duck laughs
and smiles wide.
Then asks,

47